What Moves Is Not the Wind

The Wesleyan Poetry Program : Volume 99

WHAT
MOVES
IS
NOT
THE
WIND,

BY JAMES NOLAN

WESLEYAN UNIVERSITY PRESS, MIDDLETOWN, CONNECTICUT

Grateful acknowledgment is made to the following publications, in which some of these poems have appeared: *Apple Street Anthology,* edited by the New Orleans Poetry Forum, *Barataria, Calvert, The Lowlands Review, Lucille, Soundings, West Branch,* and *Poetry Now.*

"The Widow" and "Mr. Rock" first appeared in *Poetry.* "Undercurrent" and "Downtown, New Year's Eve" appeared originally in *New Letters.* "Sum" was first published in *New American Review 13,* edited by Theodore Solo-taroff, Simon and Schuster, 1971. "Cuttings from the Jungle of Land Inside" and "At the End of the Long White Corridor" first appeared in *Writers Forum 5,* edited by Alex Blackburn, University of Colorado at Colorado Springs, 1978.

The publisher gratefully acknowledges the support of the publication of this book by the Andrew W. Mellon Foundation and the Publication Fund of the Friends of Wesleyan University Press. The author would like to acknowledge with gratitude the Writer's Grant awarded to him in 1978 by the National Endowment for the Arts, and the Writing Workshop of Eckerd College for appointing him Poet-in-Residence for 1976.

Library of Congress Cataloging in Publication Data

Nolan, James, 1949-
    What moves is not the wind.

    (Wesleyan poetry program ; v. 99)
    I. Title.
PS3564.0363W5   813'.54   79-28142
ISBN 0-8195-2099-2
ISBN 0-8195-1099-8 pbk.

Distributed by Columbia University Press
136 South Broadway, Irvington, N.Y. 10533

Manufactured in the United States of America
First edition

. . . nor the banner, but your mind.
koan

for Joan

Contents

3 WALKING HOME

What Moves Is Not the Wind

1
CAVALES

Cavale: *from* cavaler, *to beat
it, or scram, especially from
the police. Derived from the
Latin* cabalus, *meaning horse . . .*
    —Papillon

Undercurrent

One afternoon the sea
slipped into his ear
and it was all he could hear,
the rush of the tides,
his head to a conch
of bells and fog horns
and that is why

he only half listened,
that is really why
he was only half there,
half with the rattle
of tongues and milk trucks
and half with the sea
in his ear.

11

Listen, they said,
your ear's stopped up,
and then tried to make
his ear go pop and
they locked him up and
they let him out but
it would not stop

and he washed through a life
that seemed a lot like
the lives all around him
wearing a vague stereo-
phrenic smile while
he churned with the currents
and was thrashed by the rhythms

growing louder and louder
until it was all he could hear,
all he could bear, and no one,
not a single one believed
that his head was filled
by the motioning ocean

but they believed the trail
of words the drowning man left,
cupped words, resonant as shells,

and were astonished as they
held them to their ears.

Blood Salad

On the beach in Ecuador
an old Chilean woman
sells fish and *seviche*
in a wooden shack with
awnings that flap out.

'In Chile,' she tells me,
'the ocean is cold and
they have killed the poets.'
At dusk she joins fishermen
who rake seaweed into bundles

of purple and green mesh.
These they sell to Japan
where it is a delicacy
'because their sea is dead.'
The woman from the land

where they killed the poets
sells seaweed to the land
where they killed the sea.
Ancient wooden trawlers
moan and toss at dock

like widows in their beds
as the sun sinks slowly
into blood salad.

Blessing in a Guatemalan Market

Standing in the Sunday market
bargaining for a bag
of avocados

it fell upon me,
a vision of the world
covered with benevolent honey.

It happened this way:
I feel the rock floor beneath me
growing at the speed of stone,

I look up,

and as if I catch a hummingbird
frozen for an instant
in the beam of a flashlight

there is a momentary
stillness upon the waters
of the infinite glimmer

of light changing faces:
a raw goldenness fills
with the buzzing of bees

washing down on the mountains
of bananas and papayas.
I can no longer see myself

am slipping out of the picture,
quivering like the quicksilver
at the slow steady heart

of the ancient volcano,
at the perfect center
of the crystalline cone:

warm breast of what is.

Chili Peppers

Wrinkled, detumescent
scarlet and translucent,
they are the devil's
used condoms
drying on the line
in hell's kitchen,
split slightly
here and there
with devil seeds
spilling out into the pot,
into the soup, the sauce:

red hot,
they are the fire
pulled from inside
of a woman
and put into the mouth
to make the dull
hardworking potato,
the modest rice taste
passionate, worth it:

legacy of the goat
in the bone honest
house of the palate.

The Animals Outside

> *The animals outside are rapidly*
> *becoming the animals inside.*
> —Peter Beagle

Slide and lurch,
slide and lurch,
the palsied man
with chameleon mouth
and furtive iguana eyes
slithers from table to table
like a live snake act

silently thrusting ball points,
Bic lighters and keyrings
from his imitation alligator
briefcase into the faces
of the old men in *guayabera* shirts,
a reef of bull walruses basking
in the milky twilight

of the main cafe
on the Plaza de Armas.
Slipping out the wallet
chained to his back pocket
he moves his slitlike lips
counting his money
over and over

while outside
a school of backpackers,
carrying zippered worlds

of gadgets on their backs,
lumbers through the plaza
like lost Galápagos turtles
and almost collides

with the nuns in sailboat hats
flurrying to mass:
a flock of white pigeons
about to swoop
up to the top
of the cathedral bell tower
to do their daily business.

Over there, in the *cerveza* mirror
I can see the tall albino gringo
stand up like a llama
lost on the dance floor,
pack his notebook,
pay his bill
and then begin

the walk back through cornfields
of late afternoon guitars,
chewing his curious cud.

Cuttings from the Jungle of Land Inside

Tierra Dentro,
Colombia

1

This is the deepest
under water I have been:
giant science fiction ferns,
hanging boa constrictor vines,
flaming scarlet proboscis
of the bird of paradise,
flapping elephant ear plants
and ostrich-plumed bamboos
all mat, entwine and braid
into the sheer green walls
of this submarine world.

I am sitting at the very bottom
of *Tierra Dentro*—this 'land inside'—
listening to the tamboura insect drone:
hot, muggy, looking up into a vapor
of my own delirium,
a steam of metaphor,
everything larger, waxier than life

nothing as it was before.

2

We were supposed to meet
on the mountain
among proud, significant stones
but like sleepwalkers
on a rooftop
we walked right through each other
and over the edge.
I tumbled into this jungle
of land inside
and you,
the edge you fell over

I cannot see at all.
Here there are dragonflies,
transparent butterflies
and white hammocks
that fan open
like lunar moths at night.

Every word I write, a mosquito bites.

3

There are many endings to this story:
in one version we meet at the ocean
blown out from separate rivers,
haggard, blistered by sun and age,
tamed, unrecognizable,
unrecognized,
dwarves of ourselves,
we stare with pointless
stranger eyes
and walk away.

In another version: the ocean
and we are elfish, moon-wise
and merrily wrinkled.
We brush beards
in an embrace on the beach
and sit down to a bottle
of life-old wine.

Young Backpacker Just Back from India

All that Michelin gone to waste:
now his mosquito-bitten face
and desert-shredded hair

are all that are left from his 3 year
trek through the mountains to Tibet.
Now he stands in the same cafeteria

he left before and still can't decide.
Is the ivory ring on his index finger
a trophy from somewhere over the rainbow

or was it the last traveler's check
of the lost and loveless pilgrim
who confused the rites of passage

with the means of transportation
and made the 10,000 mile journey
before taking the first step?

Casa Blanca

Popayán, Colombia
March, 1974

Panama hat, grass mats, mango juice
and anise gin: dark snake eyes darting
in and out of doorways, 'hey
you meester, cannabis?' flash
of silver badges, bribe the gnats
and don't ask me where I've been:
sluggish whirlpool of overhead fans
that suck you in.

Emerald deals, cocaine, intrigue
of the tamale lady counting out change:
'hot, with plenty of *salsa por favor.'*
Politico sound trucks, carbines at corners
guarding gringo fast bucks, Latino law & order.
Over the bamboo grove more rain, heavy rains.
Disguised as Thomas Jefferson, as Buffalo Bill
I look out through grille windows

over rows of wind-frayed *plátanos*
from the white house on the hill
of this bozo banana farm, no bonanza,
while Exxon executives with binoculars
lurk behind orchids & Hilton's potted palms
scanning the ranges of dreamy green
obscenely as if call girls' thighs.

Morning, noon and night, two-thirds
of the fruit and meat on these *campesinos'*
plates vanishes, two-thirds of the oil
from their stoves. Morning, noon and night
fat cargo planes load up for the States
but I am here to stay in my Bogart coat.
Let the plane, let the girl, let the past go.
'The fundamental things apply . . .'

That winter in Paris, summer in Wichita Falls
is only a bottle of rum, a snapshot, a hit song,
that is all. Something is quietly dying inside,
old ideas and fears lose place. I change face.
'Make it new' the others wrote in exile.
Home is a headline, torn cover of *Time:*
hard heart, cold feet, sagging jowls
and pinched eyes grasp at the sunset

from a window over Pennsylvania Avenue
as time goes by.

Unripened Blackberries

Blue light, black shawl,
'a dead baby's blanket'
she calls it, the woolen
one from San Cristobal.
She becomes a little girl
holding a broken doll:
a small Pieta.

Indigo lake, obsidian volcano:
Indians, children on their backs.
'Here abortion seems like pulling
up a seedling by its roots. . . . '
An ivory jack o'lantern moon
glowers down on the bony dogs
in the cobblestone courtyard.

Blue lady crosses the lake
under a black parasol
in a tiny souvenir boat.
In a dream I am carrying
a boy on my shoulders
up from the jungle
and over the *cerro del oro.*

I wake with my pack at my side
in a dollar-a-night room.
Blue light, black shawl,
dried blood, thorn scratches,
a cup of unripened blackberries,
50 *centavos,* from a small hand
through the window of the bus.

Angel Eggs

Two children are lying
on a beach beside a river
burying & unburying
each other in the sand.

Before sex this is how
we practice birth & death.
I can hear them singing
over & over as they play:

angel eggs & demon eggs
angel eggs & demon eggs.

Late afternoon. I walk by again.
They are withered. Long white hair.
Still they are burying, unburying
each other in the river sand

but are no longer singing.
Either that,
or their song is now the same
as the one the river makes.

The Old Gods

1

The jaguar in the jungle of Tikal
pounces on monkeys and wild dogs,

puts its paw through the thatched roof
where the archeologist's grand-daughters

cower in candlelight sewing buttons.
During the full moon it climbs

to the top of the Temple of the Jaguar
where it poses on the carved jade stele,

electric gnats swarming in a halo
around its head, its sleek fur bristling

with cowlicks of prana, the night
slick with saliva and the jungle glistens,

the jungle of Tikal.

2

A cat plays Tarzan among
dieffenbachia and potted prayer plants

in the silver murmur of the late
night show turned down low.

Then it crouches motionless until dawn
like a sphinx spinning a riddle

27

in front of a mouse crack under
the hypnotically humming refrigerator,

waiting for a flash of recognition.

3

The telephone rings, the faucet drips,
the stalactites are reaching the floor.

An alligator in a green terry cloth robe
pushes its way across the shag carpet.

Bat wings shudder inside Venetian blinds
and the mirror wants more meat, more meat.

Like the full moon I am known
for a light and energy not mine:

I am waltzing like an otter on two feet,
raised on the eggs of chickens I never know,

listening through a hole in the floorboards
for the senseless music from below.

Air Lift

I am waiting for the dust to settle.
I am waiting for the plane to ground.

Eyebrowless angels with ashen faces
and black scarves around their throats,
a band of fully armed El Greco angels
with silver beards and blue leather coats,
with beatific eyes and with guerilla guns
slung purposefully across their shoulders

usher me in utter panic
through mobs of angry jackals
and hyenas pushing at the ropes,
over bodies heaped like ragdolls in the street,
through alleys of slogans and sick children

usher me with ambulance sirens
celestial as the trill of flutes,
with alchemical symbols stitched onto their gloves,
as I scurry with scarlet archives of papers,
with shells and leaves, a toothbrush and pen,
into the fuming plane where airborne

we ascend into the abalone glint of sky,
my arms flung around my rescuers
who armed against the last regime
have come after me, come to carry me
home beyond oceans and mountains.

They welcome me with sandwiches and tea.
Their crystal fingers float over the controls
of the End of the World Evacuation Patrol's
cargo plane, the sad sweet chariot streamlined
like a lion with fanned white eagle wings.

As the radio intones *all clear, all clear*
twenty-six years drop below me
into an aerial map of impossible terrain,
a Dresden of blue and brown and green . . .

In these moments of the last regime
the streets a thick soup of suspicion,
faces lean with fear, sapped of speech,
shut windows and doors of this vacancy

I am waiting for the dust to settle,
I am waiting for the plane to ground.

2

THE LONG WHITE CORRIDOR

Judgment

50 years ago, while standing in his bathrobe,
grand-oncle Émile was disowned from *la famille crèole*
for announcing his marriage to a Goddamn Yankee Protestant.
My grandmother, in the middle of pressing his linen suit,
threw it in the corner to give to the vegetableman,
crossed herself harshly then went out to chop parsley.
No one spoke to him or of him for half a century.
The silence was golden: he lived down the block.

Last year Uncle Émile raced down the hall in his bathrobe
shouting, 'Where's the white linen suit you were ironing?'
My grandmother dropped dead in the bathtub, that being that.
Uncle Émile never did renounce the Protestant Reformation,
never did renounce the Union Army or his Vermont wife.
He was never one for details. They say he didn't care.
By now the bathrobe is frayed and flecked with lintballs
as he stands on his front gallery muttering to himself

like a man let out of a taxi at the wrong corner
in the wrong city of the wrong century,
waiting for a change of clothes
and wondering what went wrong.

31

Sum

My accountant father
counts pebbles and lawn-
mowers and edges the grasses
with somber precision.
His life like machine tape
droops down in a white beard
and ends in a darkness
of double red figures
which mount like a staircase
toward some *ergo sum*.

With asterisk eyes braced
he dreams of a golf score.
Report cards and budgets
are good things to sleep on
except that they flutter
and need constant folding.
Calendrical suns stand
like forms left to fill in
as he considers the number
of hamburger patties still
stacked in the freezer.

My accountant father
made me count
one day to two
and I never made it through.

My accountant father
confides in his mother
that he really has nothing.

She calls up to ask us
about what he tells her:
we place all his things all
around where he'll be sure
to see them and count them
and sit waiting in three's.
We're all we can gather.

My accountant father
lies counting to sixty
and counting in two's
to fill up the nothing
of the second hand's shadow.

My daddy. Accounted.
A hand full of pebbles.
He never was married,
divided or touched.

Winter Morphine

Numbed by cold and dumb
as the vast blank of snowbanks,
mute as a frozen root,

I cannot love you or anyone.
The silences between trees
lure me farther from the path

until I am lost from everything
out there and do not care.
Ice crystals, icicles dance.

My boots squeak through the fuzz
where bare birches lurch out to tear,
to puncture the sheetrock sky

but it does not bleed dawn or dusk.
Remains the same. Impervious. Safe
inside. No need but the needle

that marks where frost bit the heart
then spread into deep exquisite sleep.
I could lie like Sleeping Beauty

in a glass case for 100 years
floating in a fog of fake blue jays.
I could walk for days into these hills

until the glacier finds me.

At the End of the Long White Corridor

sits an old man dressed in flannel
whittling wizened birds all winter,

fantail foliage from birch and elm
to fill the bare-limbed landscape,

to decorate the empty window ledge
where an old woman places blue crystal

eggs in abandoned sparrows' nests,
giving birth to flocks of ice birds

which fly luminescently on fire,
through the artifice of human faith,

carefully until spring.

Thaw

Winter rolls into spring
as a white scroll might slowly
be rolled up into a brown one

and the soiled oilcloth dragged
across the sky finally folds back
into a trunk behind the horizon.

Out of the patchwork
of barns and farms creaks
a player-piano minuet as

joints unjam, pulleys and people
begin to move in jerky wooden mime
like the dancers on a Swiss clock.

Ferny probes of fiddleheads
fiddle out, glorious fuckers,
surprising sap rising and running,

streams trickling under cellophane ice.
Cracked shoes get stuck in wet mud
and the old mule prances in thick ooze.

Guys sprawl on stalled car hoods
drinking beer, women take off
sooty denim aprons and hair

washed fresh falls full
and yellow and lovers
sleep like good children.

Even if winter did
explain itself now,
even if winter could,

I would not listen.

Love Poem to a Lady UFO

All right, go be martyred
among the lost Lemurians
in your half-moon negligee,

but I'd rather take you
on a 6 month canoe trip
across the Great Lakes

and make love in the tall
grasses, in the long hours
of the sun while it lasts.

Come land and
let me love you.
You need to,

after all those centuries
living alone on Venus
like a small white bird.

The Mannequin

She'll talk, even walk on out
with you and although you know
her heart's in hock at the Deco shop
at the stroke of a Cinderella clock
she'll make it in the sack with you.

At 8 AM sharp she is packed
into the bus, perfumed and pouting,
with hens stacked TO MARKET, TO MARKET,
where with nail files she sharpens
memories of the night before:

the disco bar with the single
swinging door. In platform shoes
and camp clutchbag to match
she asked, 'What sign are you?'
Capricorn? Sagittarius? Pluto

in a turquoise asteroid belt?
She has all the latest records,
all the latest paperbacks,
and a maidenhair fern
to knit baby booties for.

Turn out the light. Any woman can.
Serve love in mid-air, a supper flight,
a treat preheated in the fuselage
coming with plastic forks & knives
while pop star posters hover

39

over the bed like 2 buck incubi.
Ahhh! Then a continental breakfast,
7 o'clock siren, hurry and good-bye.
Scrub board curls, Orphan Annie eyes,
magazine cover woman

O mannequin of freedom,
consumer's hungry child.

The Widow

Two grey pigeons
are tangled together
with fishing line:
one of them is dead,
the other one alive.

They are wrapped
in a newspaper
being clutched
by an old woman
wearing a scarf
in the drizzle.
The live pigeon
is peeking out
of its paper hood.

The old woman stops
each person she passes
to ask for a knife.
She does not explain
what for but walks on,
her wet bundle
under her arm.

Jazz Poem for the Girl Who Cried Wolf

just one too many times:
wolf at the cabin in the country
wolf on the subway, wolf on the freeway,
wolf on the whistlestop tour
of the obscure geographies of her mind

and wolf on the way uptown
wolf on the way downtown,
wolf when it was only the wind
that whined at our door.
Wolf in the pantry, wolf on the porch

wolf as a crutch and wolf as a weapon
wolf as a seizure at 5 in the morning,
wolf as a reason for not being there.
Crying wolf is a way not to be there.
Wolf when I came and wolf when I left

wolf when I walked out that whelmed up
inside her, and tore at her fine clothes
and tore at her throat and tore at her hair,
and ran to the windows and ran to the doors,
ran to the radio and out on the street below

and it was only the wind.
It was just being there . . .

just being there.

Unborn in the Elbow of God

in the shadow of the elbow of God
on the Sistine Chapel ceiling

Eve's eyes are fixed on creation,
on the sprawling and muscular Adam
who churns up out of the chaos:

a form with ten fingers and toes
a nose and a mouth and two hands
a body which dares to be there,

a creature, defiant of clouds.

*   *   *

Thinking twice in the elbow of God,
Eve's eyes dart dark as a deer's
peering out through a tangle of vines.

She trembles at the thunderous
now of God's touch on her shoulder,
shrinking back from the act of her birth:

better be born as a fountain or flower
a mountain, a river, a storm or a star
or flow in a molten suspension forever,

a rainbow through all possible heavens.

*   *   *

43

Not to be boxed in the box of a body,
one person one place one time for one life:
the terrible step at a time made by feet.

Unborn in the elbow of God,
in horror and deep fascination
Eve watches the love of crude dust.

Spinning in spools of soft gauze
the caul of her dream is unwound.
She slides along railings of ribs

and wakes to the hand
touching Adam's, her own.

Garden Lizards

Breakfast near the beach:
the light goes
to my head like liquor,
white dunes
of the tablecloth,

chablis of beached breakers,
her freckled face opening
as a red hibiscus opens
to the morning. There,
on the other side of the garden,

grandfather steps from a palmetto
in his white plantation suit
and hands a cup of black coffee
to my father in his business suit
who hands it to me, in cut-offs.

A boy yells, his beach ball burst.
And they disappear into glare.
Some things never change:
the taste of black coffee
and the garden lizards

that dart out of empty rooms
for their moment in the sun.

The Story of Stone Beach

Crescendo:
then an undertow
rakes through the small
smooth stones, the sound
of applause dying out
in a hushed auditorium. . . .

Listen,
there is a story
these stones are telling
as they are polished
in their factory
of foam & gravel:

the sea, they say,
that old whore,
has bleached her hair,
dry as beached seaweed,
the yellow of faded
fishing nets.

She goes down
for a pack of cigarettes.
With coral lips parted
she sways from table
to table of unshaven men,
an afternoon breeze

through the seaside bar,
with several packages
of cigarettes in each hand.

This is to advertise
her business. She
never smokes.

She takes her men down
behind the enormous rocks
which watch the beach
like hooded centurions.
In a few minutes she is
back with another pack.

And this is how
the stones know so much,
they crumble from cliffs
bearing the weight
of this ancestral secret.
So she works

until she has a carton
which at evenings,
when the tides go out,
she trades for food & shelter
for herself & her young son.
She is a fierce mother

but as the story goes,
the son must always grow up
to betray her,
to move inland
in search
of his father,

an impossible task

47

since all men are his father,
but the sea, made completely
of tears & embryonic waters,
she quickly forgets
and soon is licking

with her long salt tongue
the face of another small son
for whom she also works
until he goes off
to find his father
who is all men.

This story is repeated
every fifteen seconds
at the still epicenter
between tide & undertow,
and with unheard eloquence
the stones go on

telling their tale,
continue their moaning,
a perpetual Greek chorus,
until the sea, weary
of the sound
of her own tragedy,

turns them to sand.

3
WALKING HOME

Top Window on Chinatown

for S. K. Lee

Old Chinese man
watches out greasy window,
top window on Stockton St.
He watches all day.
Maybe he's god,
maybe he's bored,
maybe he knows my father.
He checks out people
like Confucius.

He watches sleepwalker
and he watches shoplifter.
He watches show barker
and corner barracuda.
He· watches blind
dowager princess
walk in Walgreens
with bound feet.

He watches shop window where fat
flat duck hangs from big hook

49

like magic fetus.
He watches next-door sex shop
where flesh color
rubber dildo
on sale on shelf in window.
He watches all day
like movie for 99 cents.

And it's all same, 10 years.
I come here to corner
to buy oranges cheap,
14 for one dollar.
I see face way up
like grey paper lantern,
afternoon moon
look down
study analects of Chinatown.

He sees me and maybe
I shave off beard
or wear straw hat or get fat
but he knows ideogram of street.
No change, no change
for one thousand years
and he keeps poem
sacred in rented room
like ancient oak in bonsai pot.

I carry oranges
in sack for brothers and sisters
and walk down Stockton St.,
step back through eye of scroll,
back to life of many things,

far away, but I come back.
He makes me. He put me here,
tall man who always carries orange
through green tile poem of Shanghai.

The Already Dead

The already dead are born serious.
There is really no helping them
except making love to them,
but even this they take seriously

and ask you to explain what you mean.
The already dead are born serious.
Their lives are just long lists
accounting for this condition.

Death comes as no big surprise
but as a mute continuation
of their monotonous monologues,
finally out of everyone's hair.

Me, I wake up to their world
from a place where black children
are singing *a cappella* by the sea

and smell something cooking.

Shopping Bag Lady

Half-crocked, Christmas Eve,
I offer a swig of brandy
from my own brown paper sack
to a mumbling bundle of rags
who is furiously rearranging
the contents of her shopping bag
on Fifth Avenue.

'Lady, whatever it is
you're talking about,
we love you.'

She accepts with the smile,
though toothless, mustachioed,
of a prom queen asked to dance.
Out of her World War II baby carriage
come two styrofoam cups,
wiped clean with a babushka.
'Let's sit over here,' she nudges,

lugging two bulging plastic garbage bags
right up against the plate glass window
of a glossy uptown restaurant.
The couple on the other side
of the glass from us
are having, say, the stuffed flounder
and probably talking about the symphony.

Our heads level with their bread basket,
we are going on about pipe cleaners,
mayonnaise jars, tricycle wheels

and the trash on the lower East Side.
We are wondering about the furrier
who tossed out these scraps
of mange, which we are arranging

on our laps into a sable cape.
In front the crowds whoosh by
on their way to the next place,
and behind, the silverware clinks,
but I sit here toasting the night
with the owner, and sole proprietor,
of New York City.

The Magic Tortoise

   . . . and when we rode on it,'
you tell me, years later, older,
'the earth rock & rolled
beneath us like a waterbed;
we lived on smoke, on day-old bread,
on fire water, any goddamn thing,
our ears upon the magic tortoise belly
listening to the dolphins singing . . . '

' . . . now there is a list on the refrigerator door: (1) get something for
dinner, (2) find someone to sleep with, (3) finish arranging these little
pieces of paper. Last winter in a covered swimming pool, I saw what
must have been just a huge air bubble heaving the tarpaulin up and
down with the wind. But there, I thought, is where they put the magic
tortoise I could not find again. . . . '

Today you are 30
and I am watching carefully
the corners of your mouth.
You are pushing a metal cart
through the supermarket,
down the endless canyons
of brightly colored
things to eat.

Your fingers fly from shelf to cart,
your eyes from carton to canister,
but your mouth droops
like a neglected house plant,
opening neither to take in
nor to give out nourishment.
And I think of Tantalus
starving to death in a supermarket

in a world that's one big supermarket,
which is what the world becomes
when you let the magic tortoise go.

Bangkok 1979

The clip-clop of open-backed
stiletto heels along wet garden
flagstones: 'hey, how many *baht*
for these Thai girls in tight
skirts to go down for the night?'
Dripping of rain-soaked mimosas,
blaring of top-10 jukebox, sloshing
of ice, rattling of Pepsi crates:
hallways of empty Johnny Walker, J & B,
crushed Marlboros, mixers & matchers:
'aw, shit,' red-faced, longhaired,

rolled up tee shirt, tattoos,
another long evening by
the hotel pool. This is where
Saigon landed when it fell
and all the years with placards
we were shouting over this:
giggling prostitutes, gurgling pools,
creaky wheels of street corner
stir-fry cook's cart wheeled home
through jangled neon G.I. alley,
pagoda baby crying, suddenly stilled.

And wherever they have come from,
however, why, here they are,
middle-aged soldiers without their war:
in a continent of paddy & banners
they sit backed into the last
chlorine-smelling corner
munching potato chips, shooting

oblivion into veins that bulged
with the crackling of rockets.
Glory is cheap. Especially in Asia.
O tinhorns, AWOL's fortune hunters:

better off than the bodies shipped home.

The Subway

To be passed along underground
like something undigested
through a rat's intestine,
this is more than transportation:

these are the boxcars of obsession,
Dostoevskian, with graffiti scrawl
so dense across the train windows
you can't see out, but sit inside

staring straight ahead at
the child molester in the bowler hat,
the rapist with the crooked smile,
the mugger with his concealed blade,

whatever the obsession, you go back
to it, again and again, daylight
doing a slow dissolve as you dive in
to the hole smelling of dirty nickels.

On the surface, an old woman slides
across the frozen tundra of the square,
neon beer signs flash from corner deli's,
passing life comforts, but underneath,

down here, it is running, an undertow,
a lost river of hell, trains crashing
through dream footage of chase scenes.
A trance triggered by a turnstile click

takes over, takes you over and through
Grand Central / Times Square / 49th St.:
gulping air, you exit reborn, rush on
between the faces and into the morning.

Mr. Rock

A man from Oregon, Mr. Rock,
has the world's largest
collection of infinitesimal
pieces of God kept
in the milky onyx glow
of labeled invisible trays.

One by one
we take them out,
and under the microscope
pinpoints of light
open portholes onto
the terrible lattices

of perfect intelligence:
crystals, crystals,
will & testament of light,
specks of millennial
omnipotence,
the earth's final secret,

what we, flesh creatures,
are a vague stage
in the process
of becoming:
longshot
of glory.

His lips sealed
with volcanic ice,
in quartzlike silence,

he shows them to me
and then, one by one,
puts them back in their box.

Plutonium

The blasted powerplant wharf
that no longer reaches shore,
lined with last droopy pelicans,

washes farther out to sea,
a barge of pterodactyls drifting
out of memory and into nightmare.

It's cooler now. Palm trees hula
and water, water's everywhere
but all that's safe is seltzer.

Amphibians move with airplane eyes
on slithery red webbed feet inside
the hives of deserted beach hotels.

Whether this is the world we chose,
the world we made, or were simply given,
we sit in science fiction's direct vision

survivors of one skin and no opinion.
Strangers talk like lovers in the dark
holding hands on the last boat out of here.

Man of the Metals

In habits stiff and white
as Easter lilies, the sisters
are whispering in the alley.
They lead me to the courtyard
of a dank house in the south
for a special audience
with the face of death,
arranged by a specialist
who warns, take no chances,
everything is coincidence.

There he sits in ivory uniform
among monstrous hanging ferns.
He looks like Somoza, older
but no, it is General Pinochet
of Chile, man of the medals.
His bald head, immobile, lunar,
is a cancerous hard-boiled egg
staring out behind dark glasses
perfectly round and pointless:
black patent leather patches.

His sash of luminous medals,
patria, familia y dólar,
clanks vulcanically with each breath
like copper spikes, like factories,
like cell doors banging closed.
He is serenely smoking a long,
endlessly black cigarette.
His body is shrunken but fits
inside a monumental marble aura,

a casket of square shoulders

thrown back. As with love, with death
I speak Spanish, my voice sticking
and catching inside a rusty lock:
dímelo, dónde está José Rafael Merino?
Where is the son of Ernesto Valez?
What have you done with the bones
of Pablo Neruda and Victor Jara
and where are the disappeared?

His mouth opens but with no tongue:
I see corrugated edges of a tin
can lid wagging in its place and
not in human speech but with the roar
of a troop of tanks going into gear.

Immediately, the sisters begin
to sail through the portico
throwing shut the green shutters
as hurriedly as if a hurricane
were approaching. The house fills
with the odor of ethyl alcohol
and floor polish as I am pushed
abruptly out the front door,

another recruit stumbling
through the clean spring air.

The Dissident

Arriving at the end of their dream,
he now takes the bus
to the end of the line

through miles of blocklike
identical nine-story buildings.
He lives in the last apartment

of the last apartment building
standing next to an open field,
where the infinite vacuum

meets the vast machine—
a lot filled with the debris
of rusted ducts and rotten logs

where wilderness and progress
fall speechless into
each other's arms.

He stands there flying
a blue paper kite
in the February sky.

Downtown, New Year's Eve

Flocks of white doves
with mean red numerical eyes
are swirling down through
the canyons of high finance.
Out of every office window

secretaries & file clerks
are throwing to the street
boxfuls of memo calendars
like the leaves of the tree
that money does not grow on.

Tuesday the 25th sticks
to Friday the 2nd falling
with Monday the 14th
in an eddy of clerical snow.
A hard cleansing rain

makes glue of them all,
plasters them on car tops,
to galoshes & umbrellas.
In half a block I walk
through the whole year:

a woman pulls piece by piece
out of her hair the day
of my arrest by the authorities.
The broke want-ad day in the park
sails by on a fedora like a duck.

The day of the abortion
is caught between the spokes
of a yellow messenger bicycle.
It has been that kind of year
& is now that kind of walk

through the rain.
Meanwhile, father time
sits in his paneled office
zonked out on spirits & soda,
last numbers squeezed in place.

And the faces in the windows
stare down to the street below
as in photos of those who wait
to welcome the liberating army.

Walking Home

The bald man
in the fur-lined Russian cape
stands at the cable car stop
listening to an earphone
attached by a clear plastic cord
to a big black leather bag.
He shakes his head
as with the orgasms
of an unimaginable sense.

Across the street
a bowl-faced Korean picture
framer works behind plate glass
among the serene rice paper
rustlings of calligraphies.
He also is listening
to his heart
in the city
late at night.

Upon a small screen
the greased gears slide
in & out with industrial precision.
The brunette with the pimply back
rolls over for the last time
as the fog drops and
the back row empties
out onto the wet streets
where clacking invisible

69

cables run like arteries
under asphalt, under cobblestone.
Under this city there are other
cities: worlds within worlds,
countries, voyages, passageways:
anthills of tunnels where sailors
were dragged along, out trapdoors
from brothels to the bay, waking
two days to sea toward Shanghai.

Traveler, I looked:
there is no road, no way.
The road is made by walking,
as I am walking now, on Powell St.
with streetwalkers, flower vendors,
tourists, waitresses off work,
through a maze of separate chambers
of the single human heart, a beehive
alive with the faceted phosphorescence

of mysterious comings & goings.

Babel

Tongues clamor and jangle,
wind chimes in a storm,
yammer away
at the drawbridge to heaven
in a gocart to hell.
Inside this kitchen the hiss
of secret insect kissing:
deep sea, pink-mouthed
mollusks
opening and closing
opening and closing . . .

Out for a breath of fresh air:
a wind through the eucalyptus trees
whispers everything back
backwards,
moans like a banshee
and word by word
the tower collapses
back into night, back into dream,
into whatever it seemed to rise from.

Much later, farther on,
a beach of quotation marks,
of gull tracks, of fine print
that the morning tide rolling in
doesn't bother to read.